Ext JS 6

Beginners Guide Book

By Jay Aguilar

Table of Contents

Disclaimer

While all attempts have been made to verify the information provided in this book, the author does assume any responsibility for errors, omissions, or contrary interpretations of the subject matter contained within. The information provided in this book is for educational and entertainment purposes only. The reader is responsible for his or her own actions and the author does not accept any responsibilities for any liabilities or damages, real or perceived, resulting from the use of this information.

The trademarks that are used are without any consent, and the publication of the trademark is without permission or backing by the trademark owner. All trademarks and brands within this book are for clarifying purposes only and are the owned by the owners themselves, not affiliated with this document.

Introduction

There is a need for users to create highly interactive web apps. The user interface is one of the mechanisms by which this can be done. Ext JS has numerous components which can be used for creating an amazing user interface for an app. The creation of all of these components can be done with a lot of ease. That is why most people like to use this framework for the purpose of development. The framework also provides developers with very amazing functionalities which can be implemented with a lot of ease. All of these are discussed in this book.

Chapter 1- A Brief Overview

Ext JS is one of the available JavaScript frameworks. It is used for building interactive web applications which are cross-platform. Techniques such as DHTML, Ajax, and DOM scripting are used. Since the release of version 1.1 of this framework, dependencies on external libraries are no longer retained, and the use of these has been made to be optional. The framework has numerous GUI controls which you can make use of when creating your apps. This framework has merged the Sencha Touch framework into Ext JS.

Chapter 2- Creating a Login System

We want to create a simple app having a login and logout functionality. This will be done using the classic toolkit in Ext JS 6. We will guide you in a step-by-step manner.

Generating the Application

This should be our first step. We need to use the Sencha Cmd so as to first generate the app. To do this, just launch your command line interface and then issue the following command:

sencha -sdk /path/to/ExtSDK generate app -classic MyApp ./MyApp

My assumption is that you are familiar with working with the Sencha cmd. If you are not good at this, download its documentation and then consult from there.

After executing the above command, we will have generated an application via the Cmd, To view the app, navigate to the application's location in the web server you are using. The following URL can lead you to this:

http://localhost/MyApp

You can also start the "sencha app watch" in the MyAPP folder which has been created. With this, you will be in a position to create a Jetty server rather than using the traditional web server. For those making use of the "sencha app watch," the app can be found in the following directory:

http://localhost:1841/

Creating the Components of the Login View

We now need to navigate to the MyAPP which we have just generated. Begin by navigating to the directory ""*app/view/*" and this is where the application has been generated. Identify the "*main*" folder which has been generated in this directory. This is the folder having the files "*Main.js,*" "*MainController.js,*" and "*MainModel.js.*"

We now need to prepare our app so that it will support the login functionality. Just create a new folder "*app/view*" and then give it the name "*login.*" Once this folder has been created, add the following files to it:

- Login.js
- LoginController.js

Disabling mainView

The configuration of the *"mainView"* is very crucial in the loading of our app. We need to load our app automatically by use of the Viewport plugin. This can help us in doing it. We are not intending to create our main view unless the user has been logged in. We should remove the configuration *"mainView"* which can be found in *"{appRoot}/app.js"* for the application.

Note that at this point, we have done away with the *"mainView."* Try to refresh your page and then observe what you get. You will have a blank page. This is because there are no classes which are being instantiated.

Making the Login Window

At this point, we should create our login view. We just have to open the file *"{appRoot}/app/view/login/Login.js"* which is blank, and then begin to define our window.

To define the class and then extend the base *"Window"* class, do the following:

```
Ext.define('MyApp.view.login.Login', {
    extend: 'Ext.window.Window',
    xtype: 'login'
});
```

The login class has then been defined as an extension of **"Ext.window.Window"** and we can instantiate this by use of the "login" xtype. It is now time for us to give our class some unique properties. Let us first add some additional configurations to the window. This is shown below:

```
Ext.define('MyApp.view.login.Login', {
    extend: 'Ext.window.Window',
    xtype: 'login',
    requires: [
        'MyApp.view.login.LoginController',
        'Ext.form.Panel'
    ],
    controller: 'login',
    bodyPadding: 10,
    title: 'Login Window',
    closable: false,
    autoShow: true
});
```

Let us then explain what the configurations mean.

Requires

This block is responsible for making sure that each and every class that may be needed before we can instantiate our login view has been included. The file "LoginController.js" has to be included, since it will be forming our controller to be defined in the next line. Since we have a form panel in our view, we have to include "*Ext.form.Panel*."

Controller

The *"controller"* config is responsible for designation of a viewController. And we need to attach this to the instances of our Login window. This controller will provide us with a place in which we can place all our logic which is related to our Login window or its child components. In our case, the *"login"* has been designated to be the controller, and this will form the alias for our controller.

bodyPadding

The config *"bodyPadding"* is aesthetic. What we have done is that we have applied a padding of 10 pixels around the content of our body window. This is at the exterior part.

Title

The string passed to the title will form the header, and this is done by addition of a string title as the title.

Closable

This is responsible whether or not the window can be closed. Windows are made to have a button for closing them by default. Note that we are creating a login window for our user. This means that there will be no need for them to close it. In case we make it possible, if they close it, they will be left with a blank page.

autoShow

The default setting is that windows are hidden. Once this property is set to *"true,"* the window will then be shown once it has been created. Alternatively, we can choose to call the "*show*" method.

Now that you are aware of the configuration of the window, we have to add some child components to it. Since we are creating a Login form, let us create a form panel which will be a child of the window. We will then add some other components to it.

Our final file should then appear as follows:

```
Ext.define('MyApp.view.login.Login', {
  extend: 'Ext.window.Window',
  xtype: 'login',

  requires: [
    'MyApp.view.login.LoginController',
    'Ext.form.Panel'
  ],
```

```
controller: 'login',

bodyPadding: 10,

title: 'Login Window',

closable: false,

autoShow: true,

items: {

   xtype: 'form',

   reference: 'form',

   items: [{

      xtype: 'textfield',

      name: 'username',

      fieldLabel: 'Username',

      allowBlank: false

   }, {

      xtype: 'textfield',

      name: 'password',

      inputType: 'password',

      fieldLabel: 'Password',

      allowBlank: false

   }, {
```

```
        xtype: 'displayfield',

        hideEmptyLabel: false,

        value: 'Enter any non-blank password'

    }],

    buttons: [{

        text: 'Login',

        formBind: true,

        listeners: {

            click: 'onLoginClick'

        }

    }]

  }

});
```

Let us discuss the conditions in the above file.

Window items

In our Login window, the first configuration to be added was the "*items*" configuration. In our containers, just like in the Login window and the form panel itself, the config "*items*" may be holding a component or a configuration object of the component. The same case applies to the config "*items*" as it can be a component configuration objects or an array of components. The components will then be displayed in the body of the container by use of the layout for the container.

Xtype

Every component class possesses its own xtype. This can be seen as a shortcut which one can use to create a shortcut to a particular component. In our case, the Login window has been configured with a child item having an xtype of "*form.*" Form panels are a special type of panel which has configuration options which are more convenient and can be used for working with input fields.

Form Items

The *"items"* array will also be seen. The items array has been used for the purpose of nesting additional items. More components are to be placed inside the parent component, and this is the Form panel. The nested components in our case will be the form fields which are making up the login form. The array of the components in this case is very self-explanatory. Our first component has the xtype *"Ext.form.field.Text textfield,"* a name for *"username,"* a fieldLabel for the *"username,"* and allowblank for *"false."* We then have a textfield having a value for the name and a field label.

Buttons

Lastly, we added the array for "*buttons.*" This is a very convenient way on how one can add buttons to the Toolbar in the footer of the panel. The button which we have added will be labeled "*Login.*" For the users to login, they will have to click on it.

formBind

Our button has a configuration named *"formBind."* This has been set to *"true."* When this has been done, the component will be enabled or disabled, depending on the validity state of your form. This will be an indication that the button will not be clickable until values are supplied for the two input fields.

Listeners

The configuration of the methods and the events which are to respond once the events are fired is done here. Once the button has been clicked, the event will be propagated to the method *"onLoginClick."* The definition of this will later be done in the Login controller. Note that the login view has not been instantiated in any way, which means that no changes will be observed after refreshing the application.

Adding the Login Logic

We now need to create the login controller, which is a class which will have logic to be used for handling interactions of the user with the Login view. This can be done by opening the file "*{appRoot}/app/view/login/LoginController.js*" and then defining the logic for the login view.

The file "*LoginController.js*" should have the following code:

```
Ext.define('MyApp.view.login.LoginController', {
    extend: 'Ext.app.ViewController',
    alias: 'controller.login',
    onLoginClick: function() {
        // This will be the ideal location for verifying the user's credentials via //the server-side lookup. Let us move forward for the purpose of sample //here.
        // Setting the localStorage value to value "true"
        localStorage.setItem("MyLoggedIn", true);
        // Removing the Login Window
```

```
this.getView().destroy();
// Adding the main view for the viewport
Ext.create({
    xtype: 'app-main'
  });
 }
});
```

The above code may seem to be difficult for you to understand, but after knowing more about the *"launch"* method, you will find it to be easy. Once the button has clicked, the method *"onLoginClick()"* will be called.

Let us discuss the annotations which have been used above:

onLoginClick()

Note that we have begun by creating this method. After clicking on the Login button, this is the event which will be called. At this point, we will call the server so as to verify the credentials of the user. This will tell us whether they are valid or not. This will be done in the form of a JSON or Ajax request. However, in our app, we are going to accept only input which is not blank. Once you succeed, and then will go through the rest of your code but in case you fail, the user should be allowed to provide their credentials or the details.

localStorage

For the purpose of maintaining the login state of our user, we are using the localStorage. Once the user credentials are correctly checked, we can check on whether the user has the appropriate permission to access the application view. A key/value pair can then be set up in our localStorage so as to make the application aware that our user is valid. We can then check to see whether the localStorage *"MyLoggedIn"* has been set to *"true."* This should be the case in the initial *"launch"* method.

getView()

A very helpful method named "getView()" is introduced by view controllers. When this method is called, it will return the current view which is associated with the viewController. Our view in this case is the Login window. The login click is treated as a successful login, so we don't want to present our login window. The method "this.getView().destroy()" is being used for getting a preference to our Login window and then destroy it.

Ext.create({ xtype: 'app-main' })

Now that the login window has been destroyed, the view has to be changed so as to display the main view. For this to be done, we have to make use of "Ext.create({ xtype: 'app-main' })" so as to make an instantiation of the view "{appRoot}/app/view/main/Main.js."

Adding the Launch Logic to Application.js

We now need to discuss the *"{appRoot}/app/Application.js"* and our launch function. The file "Application.js" is very critical in the application. It can be found at the same level as the folders "view," "store," and "model." A handy method named "launch" will be triggered once the application has loaded all of its classes. The code for this file should as shown below:

```
EXT.DEFINE('MYAPP.APPLICATION', {

   EXTEND: 'EXT.APP.APPLICATION',

   NAME: 'MYAPP',

   STORES: [

      // TODO: ADDING GLOBAL / SHARED WILL
STORE HERE

   ],

   VIEWS: [

      'MYAPP.VIEW.LOGIN.LOGIN',
```

```
'MYAPP.VIEW.MAIN.MAIN'

],

LAUNCH: FUNCTION () {

    // IT IS VERY IMPORTANT TO TAKE NOTE THAT
THIS APPLICATION //CAN USE ANY TYPE OF
STORAGE SUCH AS COOKIES, LOCALSTORAGE,

    VAR LOGGEDIN;

    // CHECKING TO SEE THE CURRENT VALUE OF
OUR //LOCALSTORAGE KEY

    LOGGEDIN =
LOCALSTORAGE.GETITEM("TUTORIALLOGGEDIN"
);

    // THE TERNARY OPERATOR WILL DETERMINE
THE VALUE OF OUR MYALLOGGEDIN KEY.

    // IF MYLOGGEDIN IS NOT TRUE, WE WILL
DISPLAY THE LOGIN //WINDOW,

    // OTHERWISE, WE WILL DISPLAY OUR MAIN
VIEW

    EXT.CREATE({

        XTYPE: LOGGEDIN ? 'APP-MAIN' : 'LOGIN'

    });

},

ONAPPUPDATE: FUNCTION () {
```

```
EXT.MSG.CONFIRM('APPLICATION UPDATE',
'THE APPLICATION HAS BEEN UPDATED, RELOAD
IT?',

        FUNCTION (CHOICE) {

        IF (CHOICE === 'YES') {

        WINDOW.LOCATION.RELOAD();

        }

        }

    );

    }

});
```

Let us explore what we have done in the above code.

Requires

You are aware of what this does, as we discussed it in our previous code. For our application, we should prepare the app so as to load either the Main or the Login view.

This will be determined by the outcome of the evaluation which is to come. For both of our results to be available, we should have both the *"MyApp.view.main.Main"* and the *"MyApp.view.login.Login."*

Launch

This method will be called once the application has loaded everything that is needed. It provides us with a very ideal place where the logic can be added depending on the state of the user about login/logout.

localStorage.getItem()

We need to check for the localStorage key which was created previously and given the name *"MyLoggedIn."* We now need to set the variable *"loggedIn"* to the result of the value key. If it does not exist, then it will be set to *"null."*

Ternary operators can also be created. These are used in most programming languages. These can be used for the purpose of reducing the amount of code that is needed for an *"if/else"* statement. The method *"Ext.create"* has been used for instantiation of the result of the ternary operator.

Adding the Viewport Plugin / Logout Button

The configuration *"mainView"* was removed from *"{appRoot}/app.js."* Since a viewport has not been defined, we will not be in a position to determine where the rendering is to be done. This can be changed by mixing the viewport plugin so as to have the *"{appRoot}/app/view/main/Main.js"* operate on the viewport of our application. With this, the Main view will take up all the width and height which are available in the browser. This can be compared to the addition of the line given below to the file "{appRoot}/app/view/main/Main.js":

plugins: 'viewport',

A logout button also has to be added to the main view of the main application view of our application. This should be added to the main tab of the header of the panel so that we will be in a position to access it from any tab of the application. The button for logout will handle the click events by use of the method *"onClickButton"* which is to be discussed in the next section.

The file "{appRoot}/app/view/main/Main.js" which will result will be as follows:

```
Ext.define('MyApp.view.main.Main', {
    extend: 'Ext.tab.Panel',
    xtype: 'app-main',
    requires: [
        'Ext.plugin.Viewport',
        'Ext.window.MessageBox',

        'MyApp.view.main.MainController',
        'MyApp.view.main.MainModel',
        'MyApp.view.main.List'
    ],
```

```
controller: 'main',
viewModel: 'main',
plugins: 'viewport',

ui: 'navigation',

tabBarHeaderPosition: 1,
titleRotation: 0,
tabRotation: 0,

header: {
  layout: {
    align: 'stretchmax'
  },
  title: {
    bind: {
      text: '{name}'
    },
    flex: 0
  },
  iconCls: 'fa-th-list',
```

```
   items: [{
       xtype: 'button',
       text: 'Logout',
       margin: '10 0',
       handler: 'onClickButton'
   }]
},

tabBar: {
   flex: 1,
   layout: {
       align: 'stretch',
       overflowHandler: 'none'
   }
},

responsiveConfig: {
   tall: {
       headerPosition: 'top'
   },
   wide: {
       headerPosition: 'left'
```

```
        }
    },

    defaults: {
        bodyPadding: 20,
        tabConfig: {
            plugins: 'responsive',
            responsiveConfig: {
                wide: {
                    iconAlign: 'left',
                    textAlign: 'left'
                },
                tall: {
                    iconAlign: 'top',
                    textAlign: 'center',
                    width: 120
                }
            }
        }
    },

    items: [{
```

```
    title: 'Home',

    iconCls: 'fa-home',

    // The grid given below will share a store with the
classic grid version //too!

    items: [{

        xtype: 'mainlist'

    }]

}, {

    title: 'Users',

    iconCls: 'fa-user',

    bind: {

        html: '{loremIpsum}'

    }

}, {

    title: 'Groups',

    iconCls: 'fa-users',

    bind: {

        html: '{loremIpsum}'

    }

}, {

    title: 'Settings',
```

```
    iconCls: 'fa-cog',

    bind: {

        html: '{loremIpsum}'

    }

  }]

});
```

Adding the Main Logic

We are almost done with our app. The next step should be addition of the logic on how to log out of the system, and this will destroy the key "MyLoggedIn" from our localStorage. The logic should be added in the file *"{appRoot}/app/view/main/MainController.js."* The method "onClickButton" will be added to the viewContoller and this will handle the logout operation. The file *"MainController.js"* should finally be as follows:

```
Ext.define('MyApp.view.main.MainController', {
    extend: 'Ext.app.ViewController',
```

```
alias: 'controller.main',

onItemSelected: function (sender, record) {

    Ext.Msg.confirm('Confirm', 'Confirm before
logging out?', 'onConfirm', this);

},

onConfirm: function (choice) {

    if (choice === 'yes') {

        //

    }

},

onClickButton: function () {

    // Removing the localStorage key/value

    localStorage.removeItem('MyLoggedIn');

    // Removing the Main View

    this.getView().destroy();

    // Adding the Login Window

    Ext.create({

        xtype: 'login'

    });

  }

});
```

This is the inverse of the code for "{appRoot}/app/view/login/LoginController.js," so we should go deep into it. The function "onClickButton" is the one to be called by the button handler in the generated view in our "{appMain}/app/view/main/Main.js." After detection of the click event, the following sequence of events will be followed:

- Removing the key localStorage which maintains the state of the logged in user.
- Destruction of the current view, which in our case is the "MyApp.view.main.Main."
- Recreation of the login view.

At this point, it should be possible for us to reload the application on the browser and a fully functional login/logout app should be observed.

Chapter 3- Components

Let us explore some of the Ex JS 6 components.

Grids

This is one of the UI components in Ext JS. This component is very versatile, and provides us with a mechanism on how to display, sort, group, and edit data.

We need to demonstrate how this can be created by use of an example.

Model and Store

The component *"Ext.grid.Panel"* is used for displaying data which is contained in the *"Ext.data.Store."* This can be seen as a group of collection stored together. The component *"Ext.grid.Panel"* takes care of the data which is displayed, while the component determines how the data is fetched and saved.

The first step should be the definition of *"Ext.data.Model."* A model is comprised of a collection of fields which represents some data of a particular type. The model given below shows how a user can be represented:

```
Ext.define('User', {
  extend: 'Ext.data.Model',
  fields: [ 'name', 'email', 'phone' ]
});
```

We should then create the "Ext.data.Store" having several instances of the User. This is shown below:

```
var usStore = Ext.create('Ext.data.Store', {
    model: 'User',
    data: [
        { name: 'John', email: 'john@gmail.com', phone:
'254-113-1674' },

        { name: 'Betty', email: 'betty@yahoo.com', phone:
'254-113-1675' },

        { name: 'Joel', email: 'homer@live.com', phone:
'254-113-1676' },

        { name: 'Milly', email: 'marge@gmail.com', phone:
'254-113-1677' }

    ]


});
```

For the purpose of making it easy, the component "*Ext.data.Store*" has been configured to load its data inline. If it was an app to be used in a production environment, we would have configured this component to make use of the component "Ext.data.proxy.Proxy" so that the data would be loaded from the server. We are now ready to display our data in the *"Ext.grid.Panel."*

Grid Panel

The model we have will be used for definition of the data structure. Several instances of the model have also been loaded into the *"Ext.data.Store."* We are now ready to use *"Ext.grid.Panel"* so as to display the data.

The grid has also been configured with *"renderTo"* so that it will be rendered immediately into our HTML Document.

In case the grid becomes a descendant of *"Ext.container.Viewport"* which is the case in most situations, the process of rendering will have been readily taken care of.

Consider the code given below:

```
Ext.create('Ext.grid.Panel', {
  renderTo: document.body,
  store: userStore,
  width: 350,
  height: 150,
  title: ' Users' Application ',
  columns: [
    {
      text: 'Name',
      width: 100,
      sortable: false,
      hideable: false,
      dataIndex: 'name'
```

```
    },
    {
        text: 'Email Address',
        width: 100,
        dataIndex: 'email',
        hidden: true
    },
    {
        text: 'Phone Number',
        flex: 1,
        dataIndex: 'phone'
    }
  ]
});
```

That is what we should have. We have just created the component "Ext.grid.Panel" which just renders itself to the body of the element. The grid panel will also get its data from "userStore" which was previously created. The columns of the grid panel have then been created and then given the property "dataIndex." With the property "dataIndex," a field from our model will be associated to a column.

Renderers

The *"renderer"* property of the column config can be used for changing the way by which data is displayed. A *"renderer"* is just a function which can be used for modifying the underlying value and returning a new value for the display. One can write their own rendered, but "Ext.util.Format" is one of the most common renders. Consider the example given below:

columns: [

  {

    text: 'Birth Date',

    dataIndex: 'birthDate',

    // use a renderer to format the date from the Ext.util.Format class

    renderer: Ext.util.Format.dateRenderer('m/d/Y')

```
    },
    {
        text: 'Email Address',

        dataIndex: 'email',

        // use a custom renderer to format the email
address

        renderer: function(value) {

            return Ext.String.format('<a
href="mailto:{0}">{1}</a>', value, value);

        }

    }
]
```

The rows can easily be organized into groups. The property "groupField" has to be specified first in the store. This is shown below:

```
Ext.create('Ext.data.Store', {
    model: 'Worker',
    data: ...,
    groupField: 'department'
```

```
});
```

Next, the grid can be configured with "Ext.grid.feature.Grouping" and this will handle how the rows will be displayed into groups. This is shown below:

```
Ext.create('Ext.grid.Panel', {
    ...
    features: [{ ftype: 'grouping' }]
});
```

Selection of Models

Grid panels can be used for making the displaying of data very easy. However, interaction with data for grids is usually needed. All grid panels usually have "Ext.selection.Model," and these are responsible for determination of the selection of data. The following code shows how this can be done:

```
Ext.create('Ext.grid.Panel', {
  selType: 'cellmodel',
  store: ...
});
```

Use of "Ext.selection.CellModel" will change a number of things. Once a cell has been clicked, only the cell will be selected rather than the entire row. The navigation of the keyboard will also be moved from cell to cell rather than from row to row. Cell-based navigations are the best for use during editing.

Grid panels usually support editing. Two editing modes, that is, cell editing and row editing, are used. These are used below:

Cell Editing

With this, the data in the grid panel can be edited from cell to cell. For cell editing to be implemented, you have to first configure an editor for the *"Ext.grid.column.Column"* in the grid panel which is needed to be editable. This is done by use of the config "Ext.grid.column.Column#editor." You can just specify the xtype for the field in which an editor is to be used. This is shown below:

Ext.create('Ext.grid.Panel', {

   ...

   columns: [

     {

```
        text: 'Email Address',

        dataIndex: 'email',

        editor: 'textfield'

     }

  ]

});
```

If you need to exercise much control on your editor field, the config *"Ext.grid.column.Column#editor"* can take an object of config in the field. An example is when we are using *"Ext.form.field.Text"* and we have the need to require a value as shown below:

```
columns: [

  text: 'Name',

  dataIndex: 'name',

  editor: {

     xtype: 'textfield',

     allowBlank: false
```

```
}
[
```

The package *"Ext.form.field.*"* can be used in any class as an editor field. Suppose we deeo to edit a field which has dates. The editor "Ext.form.field.Date" can be used. This is shown below:

```
columns: [
  {
    text: 'Birth Date',
    dataIndex: 'birthDate',
    editor: 'datefield'
  }
]
```

Note that the columns needed to be editable have been configured and the editor fields which are to be used for editing the data. We should now specify a model for the purpose of selection. We should use "Ext.selection.CellModel" in the config "Ext.grid.Panel." This is shown below:

```
Ext.create('Ext.grid.Panel', {
   ...
   selType: 'cellmodel'
});
```

Finally, for us to enable editing, we have to configure "Ext.grid.Panel" using the "Ext.grid.plugin.CellEditing." This is shown below:

```
Ext.create('Ext.grid.Panel', {
   ...
   selType: 'cellmodel',
   plugins: [{
      ptype: 'cellediting ',
      clicksToEdit: 1
```

```
}]
});
```

Row Editing

With row editing, editing of an entire row at a time is made possible. This is a bit faster compared to cell editing. For us to make use of row editing, we have to change the plugin type used in cell editing to "Ext.grid.plugin.RowEditing," and then the selType is set to "rowmodel." This is shown below:

```
Ext.create('Ext.grid.Panel', {
    ...
    selType: 'rowmodel',
    plugins: [{
        ptype: 'rowediting',
        clicksToEdit: 1
    }]
});
```

Store Setup

Before setting up paging on "Ext.grid.Panel," we should first configure the "Ext.data.Store" so that it can support paging. Consider the example given below:

```
Ext.create('Ext.data.Store', {
    model: 'User',
    autoLoad: true,
    pageSize: 4,
    proxy: {
        type: 'ajax',
        url : 'data/users.json',
        reader: {
            type: 'json',
            root: 'users',
            totalProperty: 'total'
        }
    }
}
```

```
});
```

A guide has been provided in the above code on how to obtain the total number of the results from our JSON response. The component "Ext.data.Store" has been configured for consumption of a JSON response which is as shown below:

```
{
  "success": true,
  "total": 12,
  "users": [
      { name: 'John', email: 'john@gmail.com', phone:
'254-113-1674' },

      { name: 'Betty', email: 'betty@yahoo.com', phone:
'254-113-1675' },

      { name: 'Joel', email: 'homer@live.com', phone:
'254-113-1676' },

      { name: 'Milly', email: 'marge@gmail.com', phone:
'254-113-1677' }

  ]
}
```

Paging Toolbar

Now that the component "Ext.data.Store" has been set up for the purpose of supporting paging, we are only left with the configuration of "Ext.toolbar.Paging." "Ext.toolbar.Paging" can be put anywhere in the configuration layout, but this has typically been docked to the "Ext.grid.Panel." This is shown below:

```
Ext.create('Ext.grid.Panel', {
    store: userStore,
    columns: ...,
    dockedItems: [{
        xtype: 'pagingtoolbar',
        store: userStore,   // similar store GridPanel is using
        dock: 'bottom',
        displayInfo: true
```

```
    }]
});
```

That is how grids can be used in Ext JS 6.

Forms

Ext JS 6 supports the use of forms. It makes use of a form panel which is just a normal panel, but with form control elements and properties. Forms are mostly used when there is a need for some data to be collected from the users.

Form panels can be made by us of any container layouts, and this can provide the developer with a means to strategically place our form elements. A model can also be used for bounding a form panel which can make it easy for us to load data from and submit it to our server.

Basic Form Panel

Suppose you need to collect data from the users. A simple form can be created as follows:

```
Ext.create('Ext.form.Panel', {
  renderTo: document.body,
  title: 'Our Form',
  height: 200,
  width: 2500,
  bodyPadding: 11,
  defaultType: 'textfield',
  items: [
    {
      fieldLabel: 'First Name',
      name: 'fName'
    },
    {
      fieldLabel: 'Last Name',
      name: 'lName'
```

```
        },
        {
            xtype: 'datefield',
            fieldLabel: 'Date of Birth',
            name: 'bDate'
        }
    ]
});
```

This should give you a form similar to the one given below:

The form has three fields as shown in the above figure. It will render itself as a document body with its three fields. The configuration *"items"* has been used for addition of the fields to the forms. The configuration "*fieldLabel*" has been used for definition of the text which is to appear near the text field, and the configuration "*name*" will be the name attribute for the HTML field which is underlying.

The "*defaultType*" for our form is the textField, and this needs to be noted very clearly. This will be an indication that its items with xtype specified will be Text Fields.

The xtype for the field of the birth date has been set to "*datefield*" which automatically makes it to be a date field. A datepicker will be provided for the purpose of selecting the dates. Note that only the valid dates will be accepted in this field.

Built-in Validations

With Ext JS 6, there are built-in validations for any type of field, and validation rules for these are applied. A good example is when one enters a value into the field of the date and the value is found not to be convertible to a date. If this happens, we will have the CSS class "x-form-invalid-field" added to the HTML element of the field. If needed, the CSS class can be changed by making use of the configuration "*invalidCls.*"

If an invalid data is provided to a particular field, then the field will give out an error. In most cases, the error message is presented as a tooltip.

The use of "*msgTarget*" makes it possible for us to configure the location of the error message for a particular text field, and the configuration "invalidText" can be used for changing the error message itself.

In the case of "invalidText," each field provides its own way of implementing it, and token replacement is mostly supported for the case of the error message.

The error message can be placed directly below the text field and the error message text customized. This is shown in the code given below:

```
{
    xtype: 'datefield',
    fieldLabel: 'Date of Birth',
    name: 'bDate',
    msgTarget: 'under', // the location of our error message
    invalidText: '"{0}" bad. "{1}" good.' // customizing the error message text
```

}

Custom Validations

The built-in validations are not enough to handle what the users may require. The configuration "Text Field's regex" can be used for provision of an easy mechanism on how to implement custom validations. With this, validation rules will be applied and the configuration "masker" so as to limit on the characters which are to be added to a particular text field. Consider the text field shown below, which can be used for validation of time:

```
{
    xtype: 'textfield',
    fieldLabel: 'Login Time',
    name: 'loginTime',
    regex: /^([1-9]|1[0-9]):([0-5][0-9])(\s[a|p]m)$/i,
    maskRe: /[\d\s:amp]/i,
```

invalidText: 'The time is not valid. It has to be in the format "11:45 PM".'

}

The example given above is suitable for a form having one field to be validated. For an application having a form with multiple fields, it is impossible for it to share the custom validations.

With the class *"Ext.form.field.VTypes,"* we are able to create custom validations which are highly reusable. A custom validator for time can be written as shown below:

```
// a custom Vtype for the vtype:'time'
var tTest = /^([1-9]|1[0-9]):([0-5][0-9])(\s[a|p]m)$/i;
Ext.apply(Ext.form.field.VTypes, {
   // a vtype validation function
   time: function(value, field) {
     return tTest.test(value);
```

},

// a vtype Text property: This is the error text which is to be displayed in //case the validation function returns a false

tText: 'The time is not valid. It has to be in the format "11:45 PM".',

// a vtype Mask property: Our keystroke filter mask

timeMask: /[\d\s:amp]/i

});

After creation of a custom validator, the configuration "vtype" can be used so that this can be used throughout our app. This is shown in the code given below:

```
{
    fieldLabel: ' Login Time',
    name: 'loginTime',
    vtype: 'time'
}
```

Submitting a Form

The configuration "url" is the simplest way that data can be submitted to the server. It is used in basic forms. The form panel is used for wrapping the basic form, and the configuration options for the basic form can be used on the form panel. This is shown below:

```
Ext.create('Ext.form.Panel', {
   ...
   url: 'add_user',
   items: [
      ...
   ]
});
```

The *"submit"* method of the form can then be used for submitting the form to the url which has been configured. This is shown below:

```
Ext.create('Ext.form.Panel', {

    ...

    url: 'add_user',

    items: [

        ...

    ],

    buttons: [

        {

            text: 'Submit',

            handler: function() {

                var form = this.up('form'); // getting our form panel

                if (form.isValid()) { // making sure that the form has valid data before submission

                    form.submit({

                        success: function(form, action) {
```

```
        Ext.Msg.alert('Success',
action.result.msg);
            },

            failure: function(form, action) {

            Ext.Msg.alert('Failed',
action.result.msg);

                }

            });

        } else { // displaying the error alert in any case
the data is invalid

            Ext.Msg.alert('The data is invalid ', 'Identify
the errors and correct them.')

        }

        }

        }

    ]

});
```

In our form given above, a handler has been implemented, and this will handle the submission of our form. The handler is responsible for taking the following actions:

- Acquiring a reference to the form panel.

- The method "isValid" is called for verification of invalid errors in the fields of the form.

- The *"submit"* method is finally called, and the two callbacks are then passed, which are *"success"* and *"failure."* Within our two callback functions, the "action.result" will refer to the JSON response which is being passed.

A JSON response similar to the one given below will be expected:

{ "success": true, "msg": "User has been added successfully" }

How to bind a form to a model

The class *"mOdel"* is extensively used in Ext JS for representation of the various data types and for retrieval and updating of data located on the server.

Consider the example given below:

```
Ext.define('MyApp.model.User', {
  extend: 'Ext.data.Model',
  fields: ['fName', 'lName', 'bDate'],
  proxy: {
    type: 'ajax',
    api: {
      read: 'data/get_user',
      update: 'data/update_user'
    },
    reader: {
      type: 'json',
```

```
      root: 'users'

    }

  }

});
```

To load the data into the Form Panel, the *"loadRecord"* method can be used, and the data will be loaded directly from the model. This is shown in the code given below:

```
MyApp.model.User.load(1, { // loading the user with
ID of "1"

  success: function(user) {

    userForm.loadRecord(user); // data should be
loaded into the form after the user has been loaded
successfully.

  }

});
```

Rather than using the *"submit"* method to save the data, we can us the method "updateRecord" of the form panel, and the record will be updated with the form data. For data to be saved to the server, we have to call the method *"save"* of the model. This is shown in the code given below:

```
Ext.create('Ext.form.Panel', {
   ...
   url: 'add_user',
   items: [
      ...
   ],
   buttons: [
      {
         text: 'Submit',
         handler: function() {
            var form = this.up('form'), // getting the form panel
            record = form.getRecord(); // getting the underlying instance of the model
            if (form.isValid()) { // making sure that the form has valid data before submission
```

```
        form.updateRecord(record); // updating the
record with our form data

        record.save({ // saving the record to our
server

            success: function(user) {

                Ext.Msg.alert('Success', 'User has been
saved successfully.')

            },

            failure: function(user) {

                Ext.Msg.alert('Failure', 'Failed to save
the user.')

            }

        });

        } else { // displaying the error alert if the data
is not valid

            Ext.Msg.alert(' Data is invalid', 'Identify and
correct the errors.')

        }

    }

  }

 ]

});
```

Layouts

The purpose of layouts is to determine how components are sized and placed in an Ext JS app. Form panels can make use of any Container Layout. Consider the code given below:

```
Ext.create('Ext.form.Panel', {
  renderTo: document.body,
  title: 'User Form',
  height: 130,
  width: 550,
  defaults: {
    xtype: 'textfield',
    labelAlign: 'top',
    padding: 11
  },
  layout: 'hbox',
  items: [
    {
      fieldLabel: 'First Name',
```

```
            name: 'fName'
        },
        {
            fieldLabel: 'Last Name',
            name: 'lName'
        },
        {
            xtype: 'datefield',
            fieldLabel: 'Date of Birth',
            name: 'bDate'
        }
    ]
});
```

Trees

The *"Tree Panel"* is a very important component in Ext JS which is used for the purpose of hierarchical arrangement of data. This is also extended from the same class as the *"Grid panel."* Consider the code given below which shows how a simple tree can be created in Ext JS 6:

```
Ext.create('Ext.tree.Panel', {
  renderTo: document.body,
  title: 'An example of a Tree',
  width: 350,
  height: 250,
  root: {
    text: 'Root',
    expanded: true,
    children: [
      {
        text: ' 1st Child ',
```

```
            leaf: true
        },
        {
            text: ' 2nd Child ',
            leaf: true
        },
        {
            text: '3rd Child ',
            expanded: true,
            children: [
                {
                    text: 'Grandchild',
                    leaf: true
                }
            ]
        }
    ]
  }
});
```

The tree panel given above will render itself to the body of the document. A root node has been defined, and this will be expanded by default. For the store to be configured separately, the code can be implemented as shown below:

```
var store = Ext.create('Ext.data.TreeStore', {
  root: {
    text: 'Root',
    expanded: true,
    children: [
      {
        text: ' 1st Child ',
        leaf: true
      },
      {
        text: ' 2nd Child ',
        leaf: true
      },
      ...
    ]
  }
```

```
});

Ext.create('Ext.tree.Panel', {
    title: 'An example of a Tree',
    store: store,
    ...
});
```

Multiple columns

Consider the code given below:

```
var tree = Ext.create('Ext.tree.Panel', {
    renderTo: document.body,
    title: 'Grid',
    width: 350,
    height: 200,
    fields: ['name', 'description'],
    columns: [{
        xtype: 'treecolumn',
        text: 'Name',
```

```
        dataIndex: 'name',

        width: 200,

        sortable: true

    }, {

        text: 'Description',

        dataIndex: 'description',

        flex: 1,

        sortable: true

    }],

    root: {

        name: 'Root',

        description: 'The root description',

        expanded: true,

        children: [{

            name: ' 1st Child ',

            description: ' 1st Description ',

            leaf: true

        }, {

            name: ' 2nd Child ',

            description: '2nd Description ',

            leaf: true
```

```
  }]
 }
});
```

An array of configuration of *"Ext.grid.column.Column"* is expected by the configuration of the columns. The same case applies to a grid panel. However, for a tree panel, at least one column of xtype "treecolumn" is expected.

Addition of nodes to a tree

We do not have to specify the root node for our Tree Panel in our initial configuration. This is because it can be added later. This is shown below:


```
var mytree = Ext.create('Ext.tree.Panel');
mytree.setRootNode({
  text: 'Root',
```

```
    expanded: true,
    children: [{
        text: ' 2nd Child ',
        leaf: true
    }, {
        text: '2nd Child ',
        leaf: true
    }]
});
```

The above mechanism is very important for small trees which only have a few static nodes. However, for most trees, there are always more nodes. The code given below shows how new nodes can be added to a particular tree:

```
var root = tree.getRootNode();
var parent = root.appendChild({
    text: ' 1st Parent '
});
parent.appendChild({
```

```
    text: '3rd Child ',
    leaf: true
});
parent.expand();
```

That is we can do it. During the creation of new parent nodes, children can also be defined inline. The code given below shows how to achieve the same effect:

```
var parent = root.appendChild({
    text: ' 1st Parent ',
    expanded: true,
    children: [{
        text: '3rd Child ',
        leaf: true
    }]
});
```

Rather than appending a node to our tree, we might need to insert it at a very specific location in our tree. The methods given in the following code can be used for this purpose:

```
var child = parent.insertChild(0, {
    text: 'Child 2.5',
    leaf: true
});
parent.insertBefore({
    text: 'Child 2.75',
    leaf: true
}, child.nextSibling);
var child = parent.insertChild(0, {
    text: 'Child 2.5',
    leaf: true
});

parent.insertBefore({
    text: 'Child 2.75',
    leaf: true
```

}, child.nextSibling);

NodeInterface Fields

You should first understand the fields for the class *"NodeInterface"* when working with tree data. Each node in a tree is an instance of a model which has been decorated with the methods and fields for the NodeInterface. Consider the code given below which shows this:

```
Ext.define('Person', {
  extend: 'Ext.data.Model',
  fields: ['id', {
    name: 'name',
    type: 'string'
  }]
});
```

Once an instance has been created, its fields can be verified to be sure that it has only two fields. This can be done by observation of the *"fields"* array. This is shown below:

```
var record = Ext.create('Person');
console.log(record.getFields().length); // will output '2'
```

Once the model Person has been used in the TreeStore, something funny will happen. You can notice the field count at this point as shown below:

```
var store = Ext.create('Ext.data.TreeStore', {
  model: 'Person',
  root: {
    name: 'John'
  }
});
```

```
console.log(store.getRoot().getFields().length); //
will output '27'
```

Consider the fields given below:

```
{
    name: 'parentId',
    type: idType,
    defaultValue: null,
    useNull: idField.useNull
}, {
    name: 'index',
    type: 'int',
    defaultValue: -1,
    persist: false,
    convert: null
}, {
    name: 'depth',
    type: 'int',
    defaultValue: 0,
```

```
        persist: false,

        convert: null

    }, {

        name: 'expanded',

        type: 'bool',

        defaultValue: false,

        persist: false,

        convert: null

    }, {

        name: 'expandable',

        type: 'bool',

        defaultValue: true,

        persist: false,

        convert: null

    }, {

        name: 'checked',

        type: 'auto',

        defaultValue: null,

        persist: false,

        convert: null

    }, {
```

```
    name: 'leaf',

    type: 'bool',

    defaultValue: false

}, {

    name: 'cls',

    type: 'string',

    defaultValue: '',

    persist: false,

    convert: null

}, {

    name: 'iconCls',

    type: 'string',

    defaultValue: '',

    persist: false,

    convert: null

}, {

    name: 'icon',

    type: 'string',

    defaultValue: '',

    persist: false,

    convert: null
```

```
}, {
    name: 'root',
    type: 'boolean',
    defaultValue: false,
    persist: false,
    convert: null
}, {
    name: 'isLast',
    type: 'boolean',
    defaultValue: false,
    persist: false,
    convert: null
}, {
    name: 'isFirst',
    type: 'boolean',
    defaultValue: false,
    persist: false,
    convert: null
}, {
    name: 'allowDrop',
    type: 'boolean',
```

```
    defaultValue: true,

    persist: false,

    convert: null

}, {

    name: 'allowDrag',

    type: 'boolean',

    defaultValue: true,

    persist: false,

    convert: null

}, {

    name: 'loaded',

    type: 'boolean',

    defaultValue: false,

    persist: false,

    convert: null

}, {

    name: 'loading',

    type: 'boolean',

    defaultValue: false,

    persist: false,

    convert: null
```

```
}, {
    name: 'href',
    type: 'string',
    defaultValue: '',
    persist: false,
    convert: null
}, {
    name: 'hrefTarget',
    type: 'string',
    defaultValue: '',
    persist: false,
    convert: null
}, {
    name: 'qtip',
    type: 'string',
    defaultValue: '',
    persist: false,
    convert: null
}, {
    name: 'qtitle',
    type: 'string',
```

```
    defaultValue: ",
    persist: false,
    convert: null
}, {
    name: 'qshowDelay',
    type: 'int',
    defaultValue: 0,
    persist: false,
    convert: null
}, {
    name: 'children',
    type: 'auto',
    defaultValue: null,
    persist: false,
    convert: null
}, {
    name: 'visible',
    type: 'boolean',
    defaultValue: true,
    persist: false,
}, {
```

```
name: 'text',

type: 'string',

persist: 'false
}
```

The persistence of a particular NodeInterface field can be overridden. During this process, one is advised to change only the property *"persist."* The properties "name,""type," and "defaultValue" should not be changed in any way. The code given below demonstrates this in detail:

```
// override the persistence of the NodeInterface fields
in the Model //definition
Ext.define('Person', {
    extend: 'Ext.data.Model',
    fields: [
        // the person fields
        { name: 'id', type: 'int' },
        { name: 'name', type: 'string' }
```

```
    // overriding a non-persistent NodeInterface
field for making it //persistent

    { name: 'iconCls', type: 'string',  defaultValue:
null, persist: true },

    // Making our index persistent, so as to sync to
the server when //reordering nodes

    // passing the new index and the parentId.

    { name: 'index', type: 'int', defaultValue: -1,
persist: true}

  ]

 });
```

Loading Data

Two ways can be used for the purpose of loading data. The first method involves the use of a proxy so as to fetch the entire tree at once. In the case of larger trees in which we cannot load the entire tree at once, the second method may be preferable in which the children of each node are loaded dynamically after expansion.

Loading of the entire tree

Internally, a tree will load data only after expansion of a node. For us to do this, we have to initialize the root of the TreeStore to *"expanded."* This is shown in the code given below:

```
Ext.define('Person', {
  extend: 'Ext.data.Model',
```

```
    fields: [
        { name: 'id', type: 'int' },
        { name: 'name', type: 'string' }
    ],
    proxy: {
        type: 'ajax',
        api: {
            create: 'createPersons',
            read: 'readPersons',
            update: 'updatePersons',
            destroy: 'destroyPersons'
        }
    }

});

var store = Ext.create('Ext.data.TreeStore', {
    model: 'Person',
    root: {
        name: 'People',
        expanded: true
    }
```

```
});

Ext.create('Ext.tree.Panel', {
    renderTo: document.body,
    width: 350,
    height: 250,
    title: 'Our People',
    store: store,
    columns: [{
        xtype: 'treecolumn',
        header: 'Name',
        dataIndex: 'name',
        flex: 1
    }]
});
```

Assuming that the URL "readPersons" will return the JSON document given below:

```
{
    "success": true,
    "children": [
        { "id": 1, "name": "John", "leaf": true },
        { "id": 2, "name": "Nicholas", "expanded": true,
"children": [
            { "id": 3, "name": "Mercy", "leaf": true }
        ]},
        { "id": 4, "name": "Cyrus", "loaded": true }
    ]
}
```

That is all that one needs so as to load the entire tree. In the case of non-leaf nodes having no children, the response from the server MUST have the property *"loaded"* set to *"true."* If this is not the case, then the proxy will try to load the children of the nodes after the expansion.

As we have said, for large trees, the data has to be dynamically loaded after expansion of a node. Consider the command given below:

/readPersons?node=4

With the above command, the server will be commanded to retrieve the child nodes for the node whose ID is 4. The returned data should be of the same format as the data used for loading of the root node. This is shown below:

```
{
   "success": true,
   "children": [
      { "id": 5, "name": "Jackson", "leaf": true }
   ]
}
```

Conclusion

It can be concluded that at the moment, Ext JS 6 is the latest version of Ext JS, which is a JavaScript framework. It is used for the purpose of building web applications in which a high degree of interactivity is needed. These applications normally run across different platforms. In this book, we have begun by creating a login app. Components can be added to an app.

These are components of various types such as buttons, labels, and text fields. This means that one can create a very amazing user interface (UI) for their apps. Grids are commonly used in Ext JS apps. Ext JS 6 supports the use of grids in applications. They help us in the way we organize, edit, and modify data. The "*renderer*" is used for the purpose of displaying data to the user. It can be used for modification of the data which is to be displayed to the user.

This shows that you will have control of what to show to the users. When it comes to editing, one can implement either cell or row editing. Cell editing means that you edit per each cell. With row editing, one can only edit per row. Trees are also important in Ext JS 6. We use them when we are in need of organizing data hierarchically in an app. New nodes can be added to the tree.

www.ingramcontent.com/pod-product-compliance
Lightning Source LLC
Chambersburg PA
CBHW060941050326
40689CB00012B/2540